LEAD WITH HEART

The New Blueprint for a Noisy, Burned Out World

MARISSA CAMPBELL

© 2025 Marissa Campbell

All rights reserved. No part of this book may be produced, stored in a retrieval system, or transmitted in any form or by any means without the prior written permission of the publishers, except by a reviewer, who may quote brief passages in a review to be printed in a newspaper, magazine, or journal.

CONTENTS

Origin Story: A Love Letter to the Whole-Hearted v

Chapter 1: There is a hole in the floor 1

Chapter 2: Burnout, The Silent Killer of Business (and Humans) 9

Chapter 3: Working On vs. Working In Your Business 19

Chapter 4 - Introduction to Lead with Heart 27

Chapter 5- The H.E.A.R.T. Check 33

Chapter 6- The Red-Flag Protocol 59

Chapter 7: Culture: The Symphony or the Noise 73

Chapter 8-Making It Stick and Measuring What Matters 83

Just the Beginning 89

ORIGIN STORY

A Love Letter to the Whole-Hearted

I spent my life chasing fulfillment in all the wrong places.

Every promotion felt like it would be the thing. Every milestone, every big deal, every successful project, I thought that's where joy lived. Instead, each win left me a little emptier than the last.

I am a recovering chronic overachiever. I wore sacrifice like a badge of honor: missed dinners, postponed vacations, sleeping "when things calm down." I believed that if I worked hard enough, solved enough problems, and knocked enough milestones out of the park, I would finally arrive somewhere I'd recognize as joyful.

Don't get me wrong. I love to contribute. I love solving gnarly problems, harmonizing sales and ops, getting cross-functional teams purring like a vintage muscle car, and finding the one lever that changes the whole game. I still love that. I'm good at that. But those things? They don't give me joy. They give me satisfaction, accomplishment, and momentum. Then I'd return to that hollow place, hoping the next win would finally stick.

Then something shifted. It was small at first and stubbornly simple: neon nails. I started painting my nails bright neon colors, sometimes different on each hand, and leaving them that way. Silly? Maybe. Significant? Absolutely. It felt like a tiny rebellion against the script I'd been handed: polished, neutral, and always professional. The neon became a signal to myself. I can be the competent leader and the strange, joyful human. I can have both.

From neon nails came bigger changes: saying no to things that didn't align with my integrity. Taking short pauses to check on people, not just check off agenda items. I noticed we were all showing up to meetings like robots, plugged into calendars but unplugged from our lives. We didn't know how to say, *I'm not okay today,* without the whole room tilting into panic or punishment.

That's when the map started to open up. I gave myself a project: What does my heart look like? I began naming waypoints, the good, the hard, the aha moments, and sketching them not as tragic confessions or LinkedIn highlights but as visual markers of a life lived. The practice of mapping my heart made something click. Those trophies and titles I had chased were not the same as joy. Joy, for me, lives in adventure and wonder: fireflies on a summer night, a perfect sunset spilling pink and orange across the sky. Joy lives in genuine human connection, in those small, unscripted moments that catch you off guard.

What made mapping so powerful was that it gave shape to something we rarely try to describe: our inner landscape. Instead of bottling up experiences as simply "good" or "bad," I could draw them. The jagged, spiky seasons of stress. The heavy, shaded grief of losing someone I love. The glittery bursts of awe and laughter. My map wasn't neat or pretty, but it was true. For the first time, I could see my own story at a glance instead of struggling to translate it into words that always seemed to fall short.

And here's the thing: when I started sharing pieces of my heart map with others, they instantly understood. I didn't need to give them a full play-by-play of every event in my life. I could simply say, "That season felt spiky," or "This moment glittered." That became our common language, one that carried empathy without requiring all the messy details. It allowed me to honor my story without oversharing and gave others permission to reflect on theirs.

That's when I realized this wasn't just personal healing. It was the foundation for how we could actually talk to one another at work, at home, anywhere. Just as every business has its acronyms and dashboards, every human deserves a way to map their heart. When we share that map, we stop operating as robots and start connecting as people.

Unfortunately, I was the queen of fine. I wasn't actively practicing this new way of communicating, but I knew I needed to change.

When someone asked how I was doing, even when I was exhausted, weary, or teetering on the edge, I would think to myself, *You're fine, Marissa. Everything is fine.* And that's exactly what I would say.

Culturally, we ask people how they are almost as punctuation. It's the handshake before the meeting, the polite opener in every conversation: *How are you?* And we volley back the same empty scripts: *I'm fine. I'm good. Fair to middlin'. Living the dream.*

At some point, I almost wished people would stop asking. Not because I didn't want to share, but because the question itself felt obligatory, as if no one really wanted the answer. If I told the truth, I'm overwhelmed, I'm stressed, I'm lonely, I'm sad, it risked being too heavy. And if I shared the opposite, I'm thrilled, I just won big, amazing things are happening in my life, it risked sounding like bragging. Damned if you do, damned if you don't. Too much or too little. Sympathy-seeking, arrogant, or know-it-all.

The English language has thousands of words, yet I never seemed to have the right ones to describe how I was feeling. Sometimes it was because my emotions were tangled. I could be elated about a business win and simultaneously heartbroken about missing a friend's birthday because of it. Which one do you tell?

Other times, the word just didn't fit. Saying "I'm sad" doesn't capture the difference between *they got my coffee order wrong, my baseball team lost last night, and my Monday is back-to-back meetings* versus *it's the anniversary of my dad's death, my heart feels full of static, like pieces are missing and the ones left don't quite connect*. Both are technically sad, but they live in different universes.

That's why common language matters. It's not about perfection; it's about creating space and a framework that lets us say, *Here's how I'm showing up today. Here's how I need you to meet me.* It's not about oversharing or under-sharing. It's about being human together in a way that actually makes sense.

I still run companies. I still consult and build and get things done. I still love being the person who sees the knot and knows how to untie it. But now I understand the difference between being productive and being alive. I've learned that we bring our whole selves to work: the family dynamics, the grief, the movies we watched last night, the allergies, the delight in discovering a new recipe. That whole person matters to our work, our teams, and the business itself.

There's a story I tell often because it crystallized what I value most. During a customer site visit in a gritty urban industrial lot, I spotted two giant turkeys on a hill. I actually thought I was having a stroke because, honestly, who expects giant turkeys in that setting? The customer warned me, "Don't get too close; they can be aggressive." I laughed and said, "Good, then it's not a stroke." He replied, "The other day I thought I was having a heart attack." We both laughed, and in that shared moment I felt a small, fierce gratitude. My brain still worked. For me, the worst thing would be losing my mind's clarity; for him, it would be losing his body's ability to move the way he loves. We were different, both vulnerable, both human.

That realization, that we are different and carrying different stakes, changes everything. It affects every decision we make and every interaction we have, yet we rarely find ways to share that insight with others. When someone asks how we are, we default to "Good" or "I'm fine," even when we're crumbling inside.

Imagine having a common language with tools that let us say, *I am here, and I am whole. I need a minute. I need space. I need help.* This language lets us care without overstepping, allows leaders to protect teams without micromanaging, and keeps the business moving without burning people out. If we can't be our full selves everywhere, including at work, then we're not bringing the power of our whole selves to anything we are working on. Let that sink in.

Lead with Heart grew out of this messy, beautiful reclamation. It was born of neon nails and boardroom nights. It was born of grief and of laughter. It was born of the moment I decided to keep my brain and my joy intact while still doing the work I was made to do. This system isn't theoretical to me; it is what kept me from breaking, what allowed me to show up as my fullest self, and what turned work into a place where humans thrive and businesses win.

This is an invitation and a promise: to yourself, to your team, and to work. The invitation is to bring your whole person to the table. The promise is that when you do, everything changes. Teams move faster, decisions get clearer, people stay, and the business benefits. We are not trading kindness for results; we are earning better results because we hold people with care.

This book is my north star. It is the map I wish I had when I was younger and louder and thought joy lived at the next promotion. It is a love letter to the part of me that wanted more than the scoreboard. It is proof that you can be an extraordinary operator and an entirely human person at the same time.

Read it like a friend. Use it like a tool. Keep your neon nails. Bring your whole heart. We are doing this together.

Before We Begin

I've read a lot of amazing books, and I'm sure you have too. Books that gave me knowledge, frameworks, or skills I could carry forward. But research shows that simply passing information alone isn't enough. Reading a book alone doesn't cut it.

- If you only read something, you'll remember about 10% of it.
- If you practice it, retention jumps to 75%.
- And if you teach it to someone else, it skyrockets to 90%.

That's why this book isn't designed just for reading; it's designed for doing.

I always joke that I'm a "see one, do one, teach one" kind of person, and that rhythm is baked into these pages. Each section gives you something to learn, a story to see it in action, and then a **Take It to Heart** section with prompts to help you connect the idea to your own life, your work, and your team.

My hope is that along the way you'll discover not just knowledge, but a few genuine aha moments you can practice, share, and pass forward. The point isn't simply to understand these tools; it's to use them, live them, and multiply their impact.

Take It to Heart

Taking time to see how these concepts apply in your world transforms this from a good read into real change. Reflection moves ideas from your head into your life.

In each section, you'll find short prompts called **Take It to Heart**, designed to help you pause, notice, and practice. These aren't assignments; they're invitations. Use them to transform *Lead with Heart* from words on a page into skills you can live, lead, and repeat.

How to Use Take It to Heart Prompts

These questions move ideas from your head into your life. Don't overthink it.

- Pause for 2 minutes, jot your answers in the margins, a notebook, or your phone.
- Be honest, not perfect, one true sentence beats a polished paragraph.
- Pick one action from your answers, circle or star the one thing you'll try this week.
- Repeat rhythmically, the power comes from noticing patterns over time, not from one reflection.

Small shifts compound. These prompts are your practice ground.

Where We're Going

So, why this book? Why now?

Because the world of work has become noisy, distracted, and exhausting. Too many of us run on fumes, burn out, or quietly disengage while businesses wonder why performance lags. We've learned to measure output without asking about the input, the human beings who make it happen.

This book offers you a way forward. A way to see yourself and your team more clearly. A way to build a common language that removes guesswork, strengthens trust, and keeps humans aligned with their work.

Here's what you can expect as we move through these pages:

- **Stories and Science.** You'll hear personal stories and see research explaining why burnout, misalignment, and disengagement drain your people and your profits.
- **Tools and Language.** You'll learn a practical framework for checking in with yourself and others that takes minutes, not hours.
- **Reflection and Practice.** You'll get prompts and exercises to apply these ideas to your own life, your team, and your organization.
- **Application at Every Level.** Whether you're an individual contributor, a people leader, or a CEO, you'll see how these tools scale across every role.

At the center of it all is one key practice:

The H.E.A.R.T. Check

What is the H.E.A.R.T. Check?

The H.E.A.R.T. Check is a two-minute daily practice (weekly at the team level) that aligns energy, emotion, priorities, relationships, and recovery. It is a simple, repeatable system that builds common language and psychological safety while improving decision quality, team trust, and business performance.

Think of it as a small daily habit with an outsized impact. Individually, it gives you self-awareness and tools to manage your energy. For teams, it creates alignment and empathy. For leaders, it offers visibility into stress and engagement before problems become critical. And for organizations, it becomes part of the cultural operating system, lowering turnover, reducing burnout, and unlocking innovation.

This book isn't just about knowing; it's about practicing. It's about weaving emotional intelligence into the fabric of daily work so that humans thrive and businesses flourish.

Our destination is simple: a workplace where people can show up as whole humans, where burnout is caught before it breaks people, and where leading with heart isn't just nice, it's the smartest business strategy we have.

CHAPTER 1

There is a hole in the floor

Companies, no matter what product or service they provide, all share the same core business goal: to be profitable. Whether you are manufacturing cars, running a SaaS platform, or pouring coffee on the corner, the goal remains constant: generate profit and keep the business growing.

When we talk about profitability, most leaders focus on the front end. Close more deals. Increase margins. Launch new products. Innovate faster than the competition. But here is what they miss: there is a hole in the floor, and every single day, profits leak out of it.

That hole is people.

Your people are your most valuable, and arguably your most vulnerable, asset. When they are thriving, everything else thrives. But when they are burned out, disengaged, misaligned, or unsupported, the cost is staggering. The loss shows up in productivity gaps, turnover, customer dissatisfaction, and missed opportunities for innovation.

Before we dive in, I want you to pause for a moment and think about this.

Can you remember a time when you were deeply unhappy at work? Maybe it was because of a boss whose style drained you. Maybe it was something happening at home that no one else knew about, a heavy weight you carried quietly. Maybe it was burnout, exhaustion, or just the slow grind of too much for too long.

Now ask yourself: how were you performing during that time?

Were you as creative? As decisive? Did you move as quickly, or did everything feel harder than it should have? Did you find yourself second-guessing, short-tempered, or simply checked out?

None of us leaves our lives at the door when we walk into work. We carry it all with us, the good, the hard, and the breakthroughs, and it shows up in how we think, decide, and deliver. That is why this work matters. When we ignore the human behind the job, performance suffers. But when we acknowledge the whole person, everything changes.

Now, flip the script.

Think of a time when you felt fully supported, aligned, and energized. Maybe you had a leader who trusted you, a team that had your back, or a personal season where things just felt steady. How did you perform then?

Did ideas flow more easily? Did you move faster, with fewer mistakes? Did you have energy left over to innovate, to stretch, to surprise yourself with what was possible?

That contrast between drained and supported, between ignored and acknowledged, is the heart of this book. When we see and honor the whole person, performance does not just recover. It multiplies.

What Turnover Really Costs

When someone leaves, it is easy to see the surface-level costs: job postings, recruiter fees, background checks, onboarding, and training. But those are just the tip of the iceberg.

Research shows that replacing a non-executive employee costs between **50% and 200% of their annual salary**, depending on the role. For managers and senior leaders, Gallup estimates it can climb to **200% or more**. Lose someone making $150,000, and the true cost to the business may exceed $300,000. That is one person. Multiply that across turnover rates, and the math becomes staggering.

According to Gallup's measure in May 2024, half of U.S. employees (51%) are watching or actively seeking a new job. The sting is that they also found **42% of turnover is preventable**, meaning nearly half of those exits could have been avoided if organizations had acted sooner.

The Hidden Drain

The harder cost to measure is what happens inside the team. When someone leaves, the work does not stop; it gets divided up. The people who stay pick up the slack, often already carrying full plates. Deadlines slip. Errors creep in. Burnout risk spikes. Resentment builds.

Even when a replacement is hired, they rarely hit the ground running. It takes months to learn the systems, the shortcuts, the client quirks, and the cultural rhythms. During that gap, productivity lags and performance suffers.

Then there is knowledge loss. When long-tenured employees walk away, they take more than skills. They take relationships, context, and institutional memory that do not show up in an SOP. That kind of capital cannot be replaced with a two-week training program. It leaves holes in decision-making, slows innovation, and strains customer trust.

The Ripple Effect on Culture

Turnover is not just about math; it is about morale. When people see colleagues leaving in waves, the stayers start asking hard questions: *Am I valued here? Is there a future for me?*

High churn erodes trust in leadership. It makes people less likely to take risks, share ideas, or believe promises. And when tenure drops, so does excellence. Studies consistently show that organizations with longer average employee tenure outperform their peers in quality, safety, customer experience, and profitability.

Customers Notice Too

These leaks don't stay hidden within your four walls. Customers feel them. They notice when the account manager leaves, when service gaps appear, and when inconsistency starts to creep in. A client who's been bounced between new faces doesn't just lose patience; they lose loyalty.

Your employer brand takes a hit too. When word spreads that your company is a revolving door, attracting top talent becomes harder and more expensive. You'll need higher salaries, flashier perks, or more recruiter hours just to stay competitive. That's another hidden cost.

Beyond Turnover: The Cost of Disengagement

Here's the kicker: even employees who don't leave can drain the business if they're burned out or disengaged. Someone showing up at 70 percent capacity doesn't appear on a balance sheet, but you feel it. Missed deadlines. Dropped balls. Mediocre decisions. Less innovation.

Burnout isn't just an HR issue; it's a profitability issue. And the cost is every bit as real as a resignation letter.

Putting It All Together

Add it up: replacing one person can cost tens of thousands, or multiples of their salary. Multiply that across turnover rates of 13%, 30%, or even 79%, and you're talking millions. Factor in disengagement and cultural erosion, and the hole in the floor gets even bigger.

The tragedy is that **most of it is preventable**.

The answer isn't shinier perks or more recruiters. It's building workplaces that notice sooner. Leaders who can spot burnout before it breaks someone. Teams that share a common language to say, "I'm underwater" without shame. Cultures that allow people to pause, tether, and realign before they collapse.

Profitability doesn't just come from selling more. It comes from protecting what you already have. Happier, better-aligned people don't just stay longer; they innovate more, serve customers better, and create the kind of ripple effects that drive sustainable growth.

At the end of the day, people aren't just part of the business. **People are the business**. And when they thrive, everything else follows.

> **Take It to Heart Chapter 1:**
> **There is a Hole in the Floor**

Where in my business (or life) do I feel profit, energy, or potential leaking away?

_____
_____
_____
_____
_____
_____
_____
_____
_____

What's one action I can take this week to protect the people I already have instead of just chasing more?

_____
_____
_____
_____
_____
_____
_____
_____
_____
_____

CHAPTER 2

Burnout, The Silent Killer of Business (and Humans)

Burnout is something that happens to someone else, until it happens to you. And when it does, you're usually the last to know.

As a classic overachiever in recovery, I've burned out more than once in my career. Each time it showed up differently because I was at a different stage in life, with different pressures and different blind spots. Sometimes it was obvious, with my body and brain waving a giant red flag. Other times it was subtle, like a slow leak I didn't notice until I had nothing left to give.

I've seen burnout in others, too. Some people show it as clearly as if they walked into my office and said, "I have no choice but to tap out." Others wear it so quietly that the only clue is a sudden change in their spark or the way their work starts feeling heavy instead of alive.

So let's talk about what burnout really is.

What Burnout Really Is (It's Not Just Being Tired)

Burnout is chronic workplace stress that hasn't been managed effectively. The stress doesn't always originate at work, but workplaces that don't support the whole person often make it worse. It's not "I'm wiped out because Halloween went late and I had an early morning meeting." That's just fatigue. Burnout runs deeper, corrodes more slowly, and is far harder to recover from.

It manifests in three key dimensions:

- **Emotional exhaustion** - the drained, empty tank feeling.
- **Cynicism and depersonalization** - pulling back, disconnecting, doing only the bare minimum.
- **Reduced sense of efficacy** - feeling like your work doesn't matter or like you'll never catch up.

Here's what makes burnout particularly dangerous: it makes the hole in the floor bigger. It accelerates resource drain in every form, including cognitive, emotional, and physical, and its ripple effects touch every corner of the business.

The Human and Business Toll

Burnout doesn't just drain individuals; it hollows out entire organizations.

- **Cognitive fatigue:** You burn through "mental calories" faster. Tasks slow down. Errors multiply. Simple things take forever.
- **Decision-making:** Exhausted brains take shortcuts. People default to poor trade-offs or avoid decisions entirely.
- **Creativity and problem-solving:** Originality flatlines. Thinking becomes rigid. People cling to familiar solutions instead of exploring new possibilities.
- **Well-being:** Sleep deteriorates. Irritability spikes. Anxiety and depression risks climb. Physical health suffers. It's that bone-deep tired feeling, like someone unplugged your battery.
- **Organizational outcomes:** Turnover increases. Absenteeism rises. Innovation stalls. Culture erodes. Counterproductive behaviors spread.

Perhaps the most dangerous aspect is that burnout stays invisible until it explodes. Unlike a broken bone or visible wound, you can't always spot it from the outside. By the time someone recognizes it, they may have already damaged relationships with their team, their family, or themselves.

My Burnout in Real Life

For me, burnout feels like dragging a boulder up a mountain alone. I feel 100% responsible for everything, even the things that clearly aren't mine to carry. My creativity vanishes. I can't sit in silence. I can't find peace. My brain spins in frantic, unproductive loops that go nowhere.

Two years into co-founding a startup in the wild west of clean tech, after three especially brutal weeks, I hit the wall. I got off a call and didn't recognize myself. Normally, I'm quirky, bright, and people-first. That day, I was flat and disconnected, just trying to survive the conversation. Every question felt like another stone piling on.

So I did something radical: I pulled the rip cord. I booked a plane ticket and flew to the ocean. I needed to see waves, jump in the water, and breathe in something bigger than my inbox. I needed to remember who I was outside of the grind.

When I told a friend, he laughed and said he'd done the same thing, except he ran to the mountains instead of the sea. Different escapes, same instinct: get out before it breaks you.

But here's the bigger question: **why do we wait until we're at the cliff's edge?** What if we didn't need to pull the emergency cord at all? What if we noticed sooner, both in ourselves and in our teams, when things were going sideways?

Burnout and Quiet Quitting: The Silent Leak

Burnout doesn't always end in dramatic exits. Sometimes it's quieter. People stay in their jobs but pull back their hearts. They do the basics, nothing more. They stop offering new ideas, stop going above and beyond, and stop caring the way they once did.

That's what people are calling "quiet quitting."

Gallup estimates that 50% of the U.S. workforce is quietly quitting, and burnout drives much of it. When people feel exhausted, cynical, or like their work doesn't matter, they don't storm out; they slowly disengage.

This isn't just a "them" problem. Burned out employees are three times more likely to be job hunting. Even before they leave, their disengagement pulls down morale, burdens high performers, weakens culture, and costs companies innovation, customer satisfaction, and reputation.

It's profit leaking silently while everyone pretends the floor is solid.

The Real Price Tag of Burnout

When leaders hear "burnout," they often think of it as a human resources problem, something for the wellness committee to address with yoga at lunch or an app subscription. But let's strip away the buzzwords for a minute and talk about what burnout costs in real dollars.

The American Journal of Preventive Medicine estimates that burnout costs anywhere from $4,000 to $21,000 per employee per year, depending on their role. Let that sink in for a moment:

- A burned out hourly employee costs about **$3,999 a year** in lost productivity, mistakes, and turnover.
- A burned out manager costs roughly **$10,824 a year**.
- An executive operating at half capacity or eyeing the exit costs about **$20,683 a year**.

Now multiply that across your entire organization. **A 1,000-person company loses about $5 million annually** because people are too exhausted, disengaged, or overwhelmed to perform at their best. That's a conservative estimate, and it doesn't even include the cost of replacing those who leave.

Zoom out further, and the numbers become staggering. U.S. businesses lose between **$125 billion** and $190 billion each year in healthcare-related costs tied to burnout alone. Add lost productivity, and that figure jumps to $322 billion. Some studies suggest workplace stress, including burnout, costs the U.S. economy nearly $500 billion every year.

That's just one country. Globally, Gallup estimates that disengagement, quiet quitting, and checked-out employees cost around $8.8 trillion annually, roughly 9% of the world's GDP.

Let's make this personal. Picture your executive team reviewing the P&L. If quiet quitting accounts for roughly 4% of your wage bill (McKinsey's number for UK companies), and your payroll hits $100 million, that's $4 million evaporating every single year. Not because of bad products or tough markets, but because your people are burned out and disengaged.

Here's the real kicker: most of this cost stays invisible. It's not just recruiting fees when someone quits. It's presenteeism – people showing up but barely functioning. It's the dropped ball with your key client, the delayed project, the missed innovation opportunity. It's your best employees quietly shouldering the load for disengaged teammates until they burn out too.

This isn't just a people problem. It's a profit problem.

If people are the business, and they are, then burnout isn't just a wellness issue. It's a leadership issue. The leaders who can spot, name, and address it early will be the ones who protect not only their culture but also their bottom line.

Slowing the Leak

If we believe people are the business, if we believe happier, better-aligned humans stay longer, innovate more, serve customers better, and make smarter decisions, then we can't afford to ignore burnout.

We need workplaces that notice sooner, that pause and adjust before the ship capsizes, that allow people to say, "I'm underwater," without fear of being judged as weak, incapable, or worse yet, expendable.

And we have to acknowledge that **it's even harder for marginalized employees**.

When you already feel you must prove yourself just to be seen as equal, when the unspoken rule is to work twice as hard for half the credit, raising your hand to say you're depleted can feel impossible. The cost of honesty can feel higher than the cost of exhaustion. Many carry that quiet calculation every single day: *If I admit I'm struggling, will I confirm a stereotype? Will I lose my shot at the next promotion? Will my value suddenly be questioned? Will I lose my job and not be able to pay the mortgage?*

That's why systems like the H.E.A.R.T. Check and shared language matter so much. They normalize the reality that **every human has limits, every human has batteries, and every human has seasons**. They turn personal struggle into common practice, giving people a safe and equal way to speak up.

And fixing burnout isn't taking an afternoon off while still answering Teams messages. Real recovery looks different for everyone. For some, it's sleep. For others, it's nature, art, movement, or time with people who refill their spirit. For organizations, it's about creating rhythm, checking in regularly, realigning priorities, listening deeply, reducing overload, and building cultures where being human isn't just tolerated, it's valued.

Because **when humans thrive, businesses thrive**.

And burnout? Burnout is preventable if we're brave enough to see it, name it, and act on it early.

Take It to Heart Chapter 2
Burnout: The Silent Killer of Business (and Humans)

What signs of burnout do I notice in myself or my team that I may be ignoring?

_____
_____
_____
_____
_____
_____

What would it look like to notice sooner, before the "emergency cord" moment?

_____
_____
_____
_____
_____
_____
_____
_____
_____

CHAPTER 3

Working On vs. Working In Your Business

Most leaders spend their days working in the business, firefighting urgent deadlines, handling customer complaints, answering payroll questions, and tackling the endless emails that keep the train moving. This work is necessary, but here's the trap: if you only ever work in the business, you never make it stronger than it was yesterday.

Working on the business is different. It means stepping back to strengthen the systems, the people, and yourself so tomorrow's work runs smoother than today's.

The first place to start is with you.

Ask yourself every day: *Am I showing up at my best, or am I running on fumes?*

Working on yourself goes beyond professional development. It's about alignment, your energy, your mindset, and your clarity.

The research backs this up:

- Just 10 to 20 minutes a day of reflection, journaling, or mindfulness improves focus and resilience. A Harvard study showed that 15 minutes a day reduced stress and boosted attention within eight weeks.
- One hundred fifty minutes weekly of activity (about 20 minutes daily) reduces burnout risk and boosts energy, according to the CDC.
- Leaders who block 90 minutes weekly of thinking time, according to HBR, make higher-quality decisions and catch risks and opportunities earlier.

This isn't a luxury. Misalignment, burnout, or staying in the wrong role doesn't just hurt you; it drives turnover, bad decisions, and costly mistakes. Working on yourself plugs leaks before they drain the business dry. Just as important, this self-work should happen during the workday, not steal from your limited time outside of work. Pushing this activity after hours adds stress instead of reducing it.

Working on Your Team

Many leaders think their job is removing roadblocks or setting the tone. That's part of it, but working on your team goes deeper.

It's about developing people beyond today's to-do list through coaching, feedback, role clarity, and culture building. It's creating a space where someone can say, "My battery is empty, and I need help," and know that's completely safe.

And safe doesn't just mean they won't get in trouble for missing a deadline. It means they can show up as a whole person. If someone wants to share that they're going through a divorce, caring for a sick parent, or struggling with their mental health, they can. They can say, "I'm carrying something heavy right now," without fearing it will be used against them, whispered about, or turned into a reason they're seen as less capable.

Safety means knowing the choice is theirs. They can keep it at a simple battery score, or they can share more of their personal story if they're comfortable. Either way, the team honors it. No pressure. No judgment.

That's the difference between a culture that tolerates people and a culture that values them. Tolerating means you can take a day off if you've hit a wall. Valuing means we're building systems where people don't have to hit the wall in the first place. And when life outside of work does knock them down, they can bring that reality into the open without losing dignity, credibility, or opportunity.

The data backs this up:

- One meaningful conversation per week (about 30 minutes per direct report) strongly correlates with higher engagement, performance, and retention (Gallup).
- Google's Project Oxygen found that teams flourished when managers consistently gave feedback and coached in short, recurring check-ins.
- Bain & Co. reports that high-performing teams spend **50% more time in collaboration and feedback rituals**, but in shorter, sharper bursts.

The payoff is clear. Engaged teams are **21% more profitable** (Gallup). Clearer roles and processes reduce bottlenecks. Psychological safety makes innovation possible. And lowering turnover doesn't just save headaches; it saves between 1.5 and 2 times an employee's salary.

Working on Your Team

Don't believe this can really work? Let me tell you a story from a close colleague of mine who spent years leading in a Fortune 100 company.

She made it a practice to hold three types of meetings with her team, without fail:

- Weekly 30-minute one-on-ones with every direct report.
- A weekly one-hour team meeting.
- A monthly virtual team-building session.

Now, I know what you're thinking. That sounds like a lot of meetings. Too many, even. But here's the thing: these weren't just calendar fillers. They became the foundation of a true team.

The one-on-ones were employee-led. Each person had the space to bring whatever was on their mind – work struggles, ideas, coaching needs, or even personal hurdles. Over time, as trust grew, everything and anything was said in those sessions. She became their sounding board, their coach, and sometimes just a listening ear. Having that safe space empowered people to solve problems, make their own decisions, and care for their needs without fear.

And then something magical happened. That level of personal trust spilled over into the team meetings. Employees started noticing when a teammate was underwater and stepping in without even being asked. They'd say, "Hey, I'll take that off your plate," or "How can I support you?" The culture of care became contagious.

The results were undeniable. Her team posted **100% employee engagement scores eight years running**. In the very same division, other teams hovered in the 60s, 70s, and 80s. And in the financials, they consistently outperformed every peer group, with higher ROI, stronger sales growth, and more new ideas brought to market than anyone else.

This isn't theory. It's proof. When you work on your team, building trust, creating safe spaces, and protecting rhythms, the return is both human and financial.

Working on the Business

Then there's the system itself: processes, priorities, and strategy.

This is where leaders often drown. The urgent daily grind pushes out space for reflection, review, and design. But without it, misalignment creeps in, duplication grows, and people spin their wheels.

Studies show:

- Top CEOs spend about 25% of their time (around 10 hours per week) on strategy, culture, and organizational design, and the highest performers protect that time religiously (HBR).
- McKinsey found that just one hour per week of disciplined priority-setting at the leadership level saves more than five downstream hours per week in wasted meetings and misaligned work.
- Standardizing core processes through quarterly reviews can cut wasted time by 15 to 30%.

This isn't about doing less. It's about doing better, ensuring every drop of energy your team pours in stays in the bucket instead of leaking through holes in outdated systems.

Protecting the Space

The hardest part isn't knowing the difference between working in and working on your business. It's actually protecting the time to do it.

It's easy to cancel that one-on-one you blocked for a direct report, skip the 15 minutes you promised yourself for reflection, or let that strategy block get eaten by "urgent" fires that could wait.

But those small, non-negotiable blocks of time make the difference between a business that constantly reacts and one that grows sustainably.

Here's the rhythm research points to:
- **Two-minute daily H.E.A.R.T. self check-in.**
- **Fifteen minutes a day for yourself.**
- **Thirty minutes a week with each direct report (for leaders).**
- **A few hours a week on organization-level alignment (for leaders).**

The return on that investment isn't incremental; it's exponential. Better focus. Smarter decisions. More innovation. Stronger culture. Lower turnover. Higher profit.

At the end of the day, leading with heart means not just managing today's chaos but building the strength for tomorrow. When you work on yourself, your team, and your systems, you create alignment. You create workplaces where people thrive. And you protect the bottom line not by grinding harder, but by leading smarter.

That's not just good leadership. That's heart-centered leadership.

Take It to Heart Chapter 3: Working On vs. Working In Your Business

When was the last time I worked on myself, my team, or the system, instead of just working in the business?

_____
_____
_____
_____
_____

What's one block of time I can protect this week to invest in "on" work?

_____
_____
_____
_____
_____

CHAPTER 4

Introduction to Lead with Heart

If you've made it this far, you already know that turnover, burnout, and spending too much time "in" the business isn't just an individual problem. It's the silent hole in your business floor, draining profits, productivity, and people faster than you can hire or strategize your way out. You can't out-hustle it, and you can't spreadsheet your way around it.

At the same time, you also know this: humans aren't machines. We don't run on logic alone. We run on energy, emotion, clarity, connection, and the micro-moments that make us feel either seen and supported or invisible and stretched too thin. That's emotional intelligence in practice – not just a buzzword, but the daily ability to understand ourselves and the people around us so we can lead, work, and live better.

The challenge isn't that we don't know what to do. Most of us know we should:

- Work on ourselves instead of just reacting to everything around us.
- Work on the business, not just in it.
- Protect time for thinking, reflection, and alignment.
- Check in on our teams, not just their to-do lists.

The real problem is that we don't have the tools to make it simple, visible, and repeatable. We don't have a shared language that makes it natural to say, "I'm at 55, yellow, fuzzy," and have everyone instantly understand what that means and how to respond.

That's why I built **Lead with Heart.**

It's part philosophy, because it just makes sense: common sense, business sense, and human sense. And it's part tool, because knowing what we should do isn't enough. We need a way to do it; a two-minute ritual, a shared framework, a red-flag protocol, a tether to bring us back when the day pulls us off track.

Think of it like installing a visible dashboard for your people. One simple, repeatable system that:

- Catches burnout early, before it becomes a crisis.
- Speeds up onboarding by giving everyone the same emotional intelligence playbook.
- Improves decision quality by grounding us in alignment instead of chaos.

- Strengthens culture by giving teams a common language to talk about what really matters.

This isn't about adding another meeting or another checklist. It's about creating conditions where people can be their best at work. And when they are, the business performs better.

Full stop.

So whether you use **Lead with Heart** for yourself, your direct team, your leadership group, or across cross-functional teams, I hope you'll become a cheerleader and an advocate. Not just because it works for you, but because you see how much better your business runs when humans operate at their best.

This isn't fluff. It's not "soft skills." It's the hardest, most profitable edge you can build: a system that keeps people energized, aligned, connected, and resilient.

Building Our Common Language

We're going to create something that might be new for you and your team: a shared language. A language that may feel unfamiliar, yet is simple enough to understand and distinct enough that it doesn't get lost.

Why? Because burnout, misalignment, and misunderstandings often happen not because people don't care, but because they don't have a clear, safe way to communicate what's really going on. Words like *fine*, *busy*, and *stressed* are too vague. They don't capture what someone is experiencing, and they leave too much open for interpretation.

The H.E.A.R.T. Check and the tools in this book build on the idea that common language creates clarity, safety, and trust. It gives people a way to describe how they're showing up without needing to give a speech. It also gives leaders and teammates cues they can act on quickly, without judgment, guessing, or pressure.

To make this work, there are a few key terms you'll see again and again. Think of them as the building blocks of our system, words and phrases that help turn vague feelings into clear signals. Once your team adopts them, you'll all understand each other faster, make better decisions, and respond with more empathy.

Key Terms

The H.E.A.R.T. Check: A two-minute daily practice (weekly at the team level) designed to align energy, emotion, priorities, relationships, and recovery. It builds common language and psychological safety while improving decision quality, team trust, and performance.

Battery Score: A quick 0-100% check-in on your current energy. Helps you and others know if you should conserve, focus, or create.

Colors attach when there's more to the story than the number tells. Yellow = caution, Orange = overloaded, Red = at risk.

Emotion Words: A curated word bank (steady, scattered, tense, curious, etc.) that makes it easier to name feelings and communicate mixed states without confusion.

(Black Bag): A signal that something personal or heavy is affecting you, but you're not ready (or don't want) to share details. Others can ask, "How's your (Black Bag)?" but never, "What's in it?" This honors privacy while explaining a low battery or a shift in performance.

Tether: A small, repeatable practice that helps restore balance: a walk, a stretch, a gratitude line, a glass of water, or laughter with a friend. Tethers offer a personal and powerful way to center yourself and return to who you are.

Red-Flag Protocol: A process for catching signs of burnout and doing something about it.

Golden Question: "What would need to happen for the next hour to go 10% better?" A reset tool that helps you move from overwhelm to possibility.

Micro-Boundary: A small renegotiation of energy, deadlines, or commitments when your battery runs low, without stepping out of responsibility. (Example: rescheduling one meeting or shifting focus to only the must-move tasks.)

Pin: A quick log of what worked or what didn't, so individuals and teams can look back weekly and spot patterns in what helps or hinders progress.

By learning and practicing these terms, you're not just adding new vocabulary. You're building a shared map of human experience inside your team, a map that reduces friction, builds trust, and helps you move faster together.

There's also a supplemental guide with tools, deep dives, and worksheets to help you take this work further. It includes how to find your own Tethers, practice each part of the H.E.A.R.T. Check, run a Red-Flag Protocol, use the Emotion Word Bank, map your energy on the Battery Scale, and complete a burnout self-checklist.

CHAPTER 5

The H.E.A.R.T. Check

If your Battery tells you how much charge you have, your Emotion Word shows the quality of that charge, Alignment focuses it, and Relationships connect it, then Tethers keep you from drifting when things get tough.

It's simple, it's human, and it's practical.

We live in a world where most people can tell you their phone's exact battery percentage at any moment, but almost no one can tell you their own. We show up to work with tired brains, packed calendars, and quiet personal battles, then try to push through until we burn out. What if, instead of guessing, we had a simple language that made it easy to say, "Here's where I am today," and know what to do about it?

This is what the H.E.A.R.T. Check gives us.

It's a two-minute daily practice that aligns energy, emotion, priorities, relationships, and recovery. Think of it as a compass for individuals, a rhythm for teams, and a culture-shaping tool for leaders.

Let's check in with our H.E.A.R.T. and start building a way of working that makes us stronger, together.

The H.E.A.R.T. Check

H – How's my battery?

- A quick energy check, because not every day starts at 100%.

E – Emotion Words.

- Name what you're feeling so you can work with it, not against it.

A – Alignment.

- Identify your must-moves and ask for support when things go off track.

R – Relationships.

- Strengthen connections through tailored touchpoints and whole-person check-ins.

T – Tether.

- Recharge in the moment with micro-practices that keep you centered.

IRL Fun Example: H.E.A.R.T. Check in Action (from a friend)

Let's imagine a day when things aren't going so smoothly.

H – How's My Battery?

"I'm at 10% / Red. Danger zone. Running on fumes."

E – Emotion Words.

"Today I'm feeling throat-punchy (irritated) and frazzled. Not my best self."

A – Alignment.

"What absolutely has to get done? Just one thing: I need to send that contract by noon. Everything else can wait."

R – Relationships.

"Who do I need to connect with? Honestly, I need to call a friend, not for business, but to make sure my perspective is still rational."

T – Tether.

Laughing with my friend about whether sending a glitter-filled thank-you card is a terrible or brilliant idea, and imagining how long it would take them to clean it out of every nook and cranny, is oddly restorative. Humor resets me.

Why It Works

In less than two minutes, I've mapped out my energy (low), my state (irritated), my priority (one contract), my relationship needs (support), and my tether (humor). Without the H.E.A.R.T. Check, I might have powered through on fumes and snapped at a teammate. With it, I've named where I'm at, narrowed my focus, and taken a micro-reset to keep moving forward.

It's fast, repeatable, and gives individuals and teams a shared language to stay energized, connected, and focused.

Let's Dig In!

The Battery

Most of us carry a cell phone, and if you're like me, you always know the exact percentage of charge left. At 100%, you feel confident that whatever the day throws at you, your phone can handle it. Drop below 40%, and concern sets in. You switch to battery saver mode, close apps, stop streaming, and maybe even carry a backup charger.

But here's the question I never used to ask: what about my own battery?

Before I began this journey, I didn't think about my energy until it was gone. Some mornings I'd wake up already tired. By mid-afternoon, after six hours of back-to-back calls, my brain felt foggy and could only focus on whatever task sat right in front of me.

Over time, I started noticing patterns:

- **What drained me:** back-to-back meetings, busy work, math (my nemesis), too much peopling (hello, introvert life), or repeating myself for the 47th time.
- **What fueled me:** projects that required creativity, tight-spot problem-solving, or collaborating with colleagues who thought differently and sparked new ideas. Those things didn't just avoid draining me; they recharged me in real time.

Nobody shows up at 100% every day. And that's not just okay, it's normal. Some days I've felt unstoppable, running at 125% and ready to take on the world. Other days, my brain, body, and emotions were so drained that just getting through without dropping the ball was a win.

That's where the Battery common language comes in.

For You: Your battery score acts as a mirror. Checking it daily helps you spot patterns, identify what drains you, and notice what restores you. It gives you permission to conserve when you're low and create when you're high.

For Your Team: Sharing battery scores creates instant clarity. Teammates know when to push forward, when to offer support, and when to give space. It reduces assumptions and builds empathy. Everyone knows how to work with each other today.

For Leaders: Team battery patterns reveal cultural health. When multiple people run under 40% for the same reason, it's not just personal; it's systemic. Leaders can step in early, adjust workloads, and prevent burnout before it becomes turnover.

How It Works

Imagine your own battery icon floating above your head, visible to you and your team. You would instantly know whether you had enough energy to get through the day, needed a quick recharge before stepping out, or were running dangerously low.

Your Battery Score is a directional measure, not hard science. No one gets in trouble for calling themselves a 40 when maybe they're really a 42. It's about common language, not precision math.

Here's the baseline:

90-100% – Fully Charged: Clear, creative, magnetic. You have energy to give, space to hold, and ideas to run with. Equivalent: "I'm lit up and unstoppable."

70-80% – Stable Power: Present and engaged. You handle new ideas easily, connect naturally with others, and bounce back when stress hits. Equivalent: "I'm operating pretty well."

50-60% – Functional: You're getting things done, but it requires effort. Breaks help you recharge. Creativity and connection are possible, just not for extended periods. Equivalent: "I'm running, but not optimally."

30-40% – Low Power: You're dragging through the basics. You get overstimulated easily, patience runs thin, and you're likely to withdraw. Equivalent: "I can push through, but it'll cost me."

10-20% – Danger Zone: You're running on fumes. Mistakes, irritability, and zoning out become high risks. Everything feels heavy. Equivalent: "I'm still here, but it's survival mode only."

0% – Empty / Crisis Mode: Total depletion. Brain fog sets in, irritability spikes, and you have zero capacity to show up. Even simple interactions feel painful. Equivalent: "Plug me in now or I'm shutting down."

Adding Color

Numbers alone feel sterile, so we layer in colors to add nuance:

- Green = Grounded. You're steady, capable, and ready to tackle whatever comes your way.
- Yellow = Caution. You're functioning, but pay attention, your reserves are running low.
- Orange = Overloaded. You're running hot, stretched thin, and vulnerable to mistakes.
- Red = At Risk. You're in the danger zone. Your performance, health, and relationships are all at risk if you keep pushing.

These colors help translate numbers into experience. Not everyone's 55 feels identical, but saying "I'm 55/Yellow, feeling fuzzy" gives your team an immediate sense of how to work with you today.

Why It Matters

Your Battery Score acts as a mirror. It shows you where you are and tells your team how to meet you there. Running low doesn't make you weak, and running high doesn't make you a superhero. It's simply a tool for alignment.

Just like our phones, humans can run too many apps at once. We can push without recharging until the screen goes black. The Battery Check-in serves as that crucial notification: "You're at 20%. Time to plug in."

And sometimes, a quick tether, a breath, a laugh, or a Coke on a park bench is all it takes to get back online.

10% Danger Zone Example

I'm at **10% / Red**. I've been in back-to-back meetings since 7 a.m., skipped lunch, and my brain feels like static fuzz.

Emotion words? Foggy and irritable. Alignment is tough, but there's one must-move: submit the expense report before finance closes.

Relationships? I'll need to let my manager know I'm running low so expectations are clear.

Tether? Step outside, grab a bottle of water, and take five minutes to breathe before the next call. Right now, it's survival mode only, but that small reset might keep me from snapping at a teammate.

Equivalent: *"I'm still here, but it's survival mode only."*

Emotion Words

If the Battery Score tells us how much energy you have, the Emotion Word tells us what kind of energy it is. Together, they paint a fuller picture of how you're showing up to work today.

Why does this matter? Because "fine" doesn't tell us anything. A 65% battery can look completely different depending on whether you're curious, steady, anxious, scattered, or inspired. Naming an emotion creates clarity, and clarity drives empathy and smarter decisions.

- **For you:** Naming emotions builds self-awareness, a core pillar of emotional intelligence (EQ). Instead of letting feelings run in the background, you acknowledge them, which helps you regulate them.
- **For your team:** Sharing emotions reduces guesswork. People know whether you're in a good space to brainstorm, need focus time, or could use a little grace.
- **For leaders:** It surfaces patterns. If the team is collectively "tense" or "foggy," that's a signal to pause, recalibrate, and offer support in a different way.

The goal isn't to turn meetings into therapy or justify poor performance. It's to give everyone a common language to say, "I'm here, and this is the state I'm bringing with me today." That simple act transforms how we work together: faster understanding, fewer assumptions, and more trust.

Emotion Words Example

"I'm at **65% / Yellow**. On paper, that's functional. I can get through the day. But my emotion words are **anxious and scattered**. That tells a different story.

Alignment: My must-move is finishing the client draft, but with my brain feeling all over the place, I know it will take extra focus.

Relationships: I'll give my team a heads-up that I might be slower to respond today, so they don't mistake silence for disinterest.

Tether: Ten minutes of journaling to dump out the noise before I dive into work.

The battery number says I've got enough in the tank, but the emotion words tell me how I'll need to drive it."

Alignment

If your Battery shows how much energy you have, and your color and Emotion Word show the flavor of that energy, Alignment points that energy in the right direction. It asks, "What are the one to three must-moves today that actually connect to my role and goals?"

Why does this matter? Because misalignment is one of the fastest paths to burnout. We spend hours on tasks, emails, or fire drills that don't ladder up to what really matters, then wonder why we're drained but not fulfilled.

- **For you:** Alignment helps cut through the noise. Instead of juggling twelve competing priorities, you identify the few things that truly move the needle. That focus gives your day shape and purpose.
- **For your team:** Alignment creates transparency. When everyone knows what each person is moving forward with, duplication drops and collaboration rises.
- **For leaders:** It's a diagnostic tool. When an entire team struggles to name clear must-moves, it reveals role confusion, unclear strategy, or misaligned priorities.

The power of Alignment isn't in creating a perfect list. It's in asking yourself daily, *"Am I spending my energy on what matters most?"* When battery, emotion, and alignment work together, you're not just showing up; you're showing up with purpose.

Alignment Example

"I'm at **55% / Orange.** Enough to function, but not enough to spread thin. Emotion words? **Tired but determined.**

Here's where Alignment matters. I've got ten things on my list, but only three truly move the needle today:

finalizing the budget draft, prepping for tomorrow's client call, and giving feedback to my direct report. The rest can wait.

Without alignment, I'd scatter my low battery across busy work and end the day even more drained. With it, I know exactly where to direct my limited energy, and that's the difference between *being busy and making progress*.

Relationships

If your Battery shows your energy, your Emotion Word reveals your state, and Alignment clarifies your priorities, then Relationships ask, "Who needs a touchpoint today?" Sometimes, *"Who do I need a touchpoint with?" isn't about who needs something from me; it's about who I need to function*, especially when my battery is low.

Work isn't just about tasks; it's about people. Customers, peers, direct reports, and leaders all depend on connection. When those connections weaken, trust, momentum, and collaboration suffer.

- **For you:** Relationships remind you that you don't work alone. One check-in, thank-you, or quick update often keeps things moving with less effort than trying to handle everything yourself.

- **For your team:** Regular touchpoints stop small disconnects from becoming big problems. They also build a culture of care, where people feel valued beyond their outputs.
- **For leaders:** Relationship check-ins reveal patterns. When three people flag low batteries tied to the same person or process, that's your signal to step in and remove the blocker.

Relationships also recognize that people connect differently. Some thrive on coffee chats, others prefer quick Slack messages, and others connect through shared wins in team meetings. When touchpoints match someone's style, they build trust. When they don't, they create friction.

This step reminds us that work gets done through people. Investing in just one intentional relationship touchpoint each day compounds over time—in trust, speed, and results.

Relationships Example

"**I'm at 40% / Yellow.** Not my worst day, but my energy is thin. Emotion words? **Drained and scattered**.

For Relationships, I can see both sides. **Push:** my teammate just landed a big client win, and even at 40% I can send a quick note of congratulations. That small nudge strengthens the connection without draining me further. **Pull:** I also know I need grounding, so I'll reach out to a trusted colleague for a five-minute reset. Just hearing "You've got this" will help me keep moving.

Relationships in the H.E.A.R.T. Check aren't only about who needs me. Sometimes it's about naming who I need and building the safety to ask.

(High Battery)

"I'm at 90% / Green. I slept well, my head is clear, and I have lots of energy to give. Emotion words? **Grounded and steady**.

On days like this, Relationships are where I can lean outward. A teammate has been running close to empty all week, so I'll check in and offer to cover their afternoon call. Another colleague mentioned feeling stuck on a project, and I've got the bandwidth to brainstorm with them.

When my battery is high, I don't just protect my own focus; I can extend it. Relationships become less about who I need and more about who I can hold space for. That's when culture gets stronger, because everyone knows there will be days they'll be on the receiving end too."

Tethers

If your **Battery** shows how much charge you have, your **Emotion Word** reveals the quality of that charge,

Alignment focuses it, and **Relationships** connect it, then **Tethers** are what keep you from drifting when things get tough.

A Tether is a small, repeatable practice that helps you restore balance. It doesn't need to fix everything; it just needs to bring you a little closer to steady. Sometimes that's a 10% lift, and sometimes it's the choice that stops you from running on empty.

- **For you:** Tethers give you agency. Instead of spiraling into depletion, you can reach for something simple and grounding, a breath, a walk, a laugh, or a Coke on a park bench.
- **For your team:** When everyone has their own Tether menu, they recharge in ways that fit them. What fuels one person might drain another, and that's okay.
- **For leaders:** Encouraging Tethers normalizes self-care as part of performance. It says, *"We'd rather you pause for two minutes now than burn out for two months later."*

Physiologically, Tethers reset your nervous system. Emotionally, they release the chemicals of connection and joy. Psychologically, they restore a sense of control. A Tether at 2:55 p.m. can be as powerful as a 3:00 coffee, a perfectly timed text, or two minutes in the sun. It's not about solving everything; it's about anchoring yourself so you can keep moving forward.

Chasing Sunbeams: My First Tether

The first time I realized that a simple action could break the relentless stream of Teams messages, emails, and never-ending to-do lists was when I discovered something called a sun break.

Back when my team's call center was in Tacoma, Washington, I once called for help with an issue and heard, *"Everyone's out for a sun break."* Raised in Florida and later living in Kansas, I couldn't wrap my head around it. I'd never known a shortage of sun. Why would anyone walk away from work in the middle of the day just to stand outside in the light?

Years later, after moving to that same city, I got it. One fall afternoon, deep in year-end pricing, the most grueling, math-heavy, high-stakes work we did all year, the sun broke through. People left their desks, drifted outside, and without much talking, simply turned their faces upward. Human sundials.

That day, I joined them. The damp air, the crisp breeze, the sudden warmth cutting through the cold, for those few minutes, my brain went quiet. And in that quiet, something clicked. I solved a pricing problem I had been wrestling with for weeks, a solution that eventually reshaped how we handled market pricing and affected hundreds of thousands of workers.

The lesson wasn't just about the numbers. It was about the sun, about stepping outside, touching the earth, and letting the noise fall away. That day taught me the power of a Tether.

Why Tethers Work

Tethers don't have to be big or dramatic. Mine is stepping outside. Yours might be stretching, journaling for two minutes, or laughing with a friend. The point isn't what it looks like; it's that it works for you.

Here's why:

- **Physiologically:** Breathing, moving, or hydrating resets your nervous system.
- **Emotionally:** Gratitude, humor, or connection spark dopamine, oxytocin, and serotonin, the brain's natural lift.
- **Psychologically:** Quick wins, like clearing your inbox, restore a sense of control and momentum.

When your battery is low, small shifts feel big. A two-minute walk, a Coke on a park bench, box breathing, meditation, or a perfectly timed text from a friend — none of these fix everything, but they can move you closer to steadiness. And sometimes, 10% is enough to keep going.

Finding Your Tethers

Your Tethers will change over time, and that's normal. What grounds you today may not be what you need a year from now. What matters is knowing them, tracking them, and using them on purpose.

Think of them as your personal battery pack, always available and always enough to bring you back to yourself. At work, at home, or in the middle of overwhelm, your Tethers are the line you grab to stop drifting and return to center.

The (Black Bag)

The **(Black Bag)** is something you can tack onto the end of your battery score, color, and emotion word to signal that you're carrying something heavy or personal that's affecting you, but you don't want to share the details.

It's not an invitation to probe. What's inside isn't meant to be opened, questioned, or analyzed. It's simply a boundary that protects your privacy and dignity. Saying "(Black Bag)" gives context for why your battery might be low or your focus might be off, without forcing you to share the backstory.

This matters because it:

- Removes the pressure to retell trauma or private events just to get support.

- Stops teams from guessing, prodding, or misreading performance dips.
- Creates immediate psychological safety and acknowledgment without extraction.
- Preserves your energy so you can function without reliving the pain.

We use the (Black Bag) to normalize that people bring their whole selves to work. Sometimes that includes things they don't want to put on display. By naming that space, we create a way to be honest without oversharing.

Here's what you need to know now: when describing your battery score, color, and emotion word, if you're carrying something you'd rather not talk about, you can simply add "(Black Bag)" to the end. Everyone will know exactly what you mean.

Later in the book, you'll learn how to use the (Black Bag) in practice during H.E.A.R.T. check-ins as a leader, a teammate, and for yourself. For now, what matters is understanding that it's a tool for safety, dignity, and clarity when words feel too heavy.

Example: (Black Bag)

On paper, things look amazing. You just crushed a big presentation, closed the deal everyone's been chasing, and the team expects you to be riding high. Instead, you're quieter than usual. They're worried, wondering if something's wrong at work, maybe layoffs, maybe bad news you haven't shared.

What they can't see is that outside of work, life feels heavy. You're running two teenagers between competitive sports, managing aging parents who suddenly need more of you, and in the middle of it all, you've lost track of what you need. You're not ready to open that up at work yet; it feels too raw, too personal.

So in your H.E.A.R.T. check-in, you say:

"I'm 55/Orange, steady but carrying a (Black Bag)."

That's enough. The team knows it's not about work performance, and they don't have to guess. They don't press or pry. They simply hold space, trust you, and keep the culture safe until you're ready, if you're ever ready, to share more.

The (Black Bag) in My Life

A few years ago, my dad was dying. Both of my parents were in the hospital at the same time, my mom battling a catastrophic COPD flare, my dad in the ICU with no hope of recovery. The doctors said he wouldn't get better, and we decided to bring him home to hospice so he could pass in peace.

What followed were some of the hardest days I've ever lived.

By day, I was consulting full-time. By night, I was making meals, managing medications, coordinating with hospice, and sitting with my dad as friends and family came to say their goodbyes. I was the daughter, the nurse, the cook, the messenger. I carried the weight of a thousand decisions, or at least it felt like they were all mine to make.

And all the while, I was still on conference calls, still showing up for my team, still answering texts from friends who loved me and wanted to check in.

Here's the thing: their intentions were beautiful. They wanted to know how they could help, to hear how my dad was doing, to offer love and support. But I couldn't bear retelling the story one more time. I couldn't explain again that he was in pain, shaking, asking to die. I couldn't say that the only dad I ever knew was slipping through my fingers, unrecognizable yet somehow still the man who raised me.

Every time I put words to it, it tore me open again.

What I needed wasn't another round of questions or sympathy. What I needed was a way to say, "Something enormous is happening. *I'm carrying it. I can't talk about it right now, but please don't mistake my silence for not needing care.*"

That's what the (Black Bag) is for.

If I'd had this language then, I could have told my colleagues and friends, "Today I'm a 0/Red (Black Bag)." No details. No retelling. No need to choose between silence and oversharing. Just a clear signal: I'm here, I'm struggling, and I'm carrying something too heavy to open right now.

The (Black Bag) would have given me dignity. It would have honored my grief without demanding I narrate it. It would have let people check in, "How's your (Black Bag) today?" without pressuring me to unpack what was inside. Or better yet, it would have let them take something off my plate, if possible, without asking me.

When a person is carrying a (Black Bag), asking them what they need, while well-intended, often adds to the burden because they have no capacity to create a list of what would help. When you can, just do. Maybe you know Coke Zero is their favorite drink, so you bring them one.

Looking back, I think it might be the best accessory I've ever had.

Because here's what's real: all of us carry ((Black Bag)s) at some point. Loss. Divorce. Illness. Anxiety. Family struggles. Things that are too raw, too private, or too complicated to share in the moment. We compartmentalize to survive the day. We show up to work wearing invisible weights. And without language for it, people around us are left guessing, or worse, misjudging our silence.

That's why we need this tool. Honoring the (Black Bag) doesn't just protect the person carrying it; it protects the team's entire culture. It says, "You don't owe us your story. You owe yourself your dignity." And we'll honor that, even in silence.

The (Black Bag) creates a cultural contract: we see the bag, we honor the bag, and we offer concrete help without forcing disclosure. It's one of those small practices that transforms culture over time. People don't have to be brave and performative. They just get to be human.

How to signal a (Black Bag)

Integrate it into the H.E.A.R.T. Check as a quick suffix to H/E:

- "H: 22/Red (Black Bag)"
- "E: heavy (Black Bag)"

Use the phrase exactly so everyone knows the meaning.

Example scripts (copy/paste ready)

Team member → team: "Heads up, I'm 30/Orange (Black Bag) today. I'll need help covering the 2 p.m. status. Appreciate you."

Leader → member: "Thank you for telling me. Take the time you need. I'll have Alex cover the 2 p.m., and we'll shift the deadline to Friday."

Teammate → member: "I hear you. I can take that client call. Text me if you want anything changed."

Take It to Heart Chapter 5: The H.E.A.R.T. Check at a Glance

If I start using the H.E.A.R.T. Check tomorrow, where would it help me most, with myself, my team, or my culture?

_____
_____
_____
_____

Which step (Battery, Emotion, Alignment, Relationships, Tether) feels easiest for me? Which feels hardest?

_____
_____
_____
_____

How would my day change if I took just 2 minutes to run this check every morning?

_____
_____
_____
_____
_____

What's stopping me from trying it right now?

_____
_____
_____
_____
_____

CHAPTER 6

The Red-Flag Protocol

Sometimes the H.E.A.R.T. Check reveals more than a low battery or heavy emotion. Sometimes there are signals you can't ignore: irritability, decision fatigue, rising mistakes, or someone clearly at risk of crashing. That's where the **Red-Flag Protocol** comes in.

The Red-Flag Protocol is designed to catch burnout before it spirals out of control. It operates at three levels: **Self, Team, and Leader (S-T-L)**.

- **For you:** It's your emergency brake. When you notice yourself spiraling, name where you are, ask the Golden Question, and choose a tether before burnout takes hold.
- **For your team:** It's a shared safety net. When you spot a teammate sliding, notice tone shifts, frequent interruptions, or mounting errors, and call a quick check-in. No shame, just support.

- **For leaders:** It's a core responsibility. Leaders must model the protocol, watch for patterns, and step in early. A team constantly running in the red signals a culture problem, not individual failure.

How It Works

- **Notice:** Catch the warning signs such as rising interruptions, tone shifts, or decision fatigue. See something, say something.
- **Name:** State your battery level plus one emotion (for example, "55%, Yellow, Fuzzy"). Note that a low battery or heavy emotion doesn't automatically mean Red-Flag.
- **Golden Question:** Ask yourself, "What would need to happen for the next hour to go 10% better?"
- **Pick a Tether:** Choose one and do it immediately.
- **Micro-Boundary:** If your battery drops below 40%, adjust a deadline, reschedule a meeting, or narrow your focus. Ask for help when you need it.
- **Log a Pin:** Note what worked so you can spot patterns during your weekly review.

Why It Matters

Red flags aren't failures; they're early warning signals. The protocol creates a safe space to pause, reset, and renegotiate your approach. It prevents small struggles from exploding into full-blown crises and teaches teams that protecting energy fuels performance rather than hindering it.

Sometimes the Red-Flag Protocol looks simple: grabbing a tether, taking a break, or setting a micro-boundary. Other times it becomes critical: calling in a teammate for backup, escalating to leadership, or stopping work entirely before real damage occurs. Either way, the goal remains the same: **catch it early, respond with compassion, and keep both the human and the work steady**.

The Phone-a-Friend Moment

Not every red flag calls for just a glass of water or five minutes of quiet. Sometimes it's critical, the kind of moment where one wrong move could trigger a devastating chain reaction.

Picture this: you're the only one holding the final numbers for a board presentation. The slides are loaded, the room is waiting, and investor confidence hangs on what you're about to say. But inside, you know the truth. Your battery sits at 25/Red, your brain feels foggy, and every word moves like it's stuck in quicksand.

You can push through, hope adrenaline carries you, and risk missing something critical. Or you can deploy the Red-Flag Protocol.

Here's how it works in real time:
- **Notice (Self):** You catch yourself staring blankly at the slide, unable to recall the detail you normally know well. You admit, *"I'm too depleted to handle this safely."*
- **Name (Self):** You call it clearly: *"I'm 25/Red, spiky."* No judgment, just facts.
- **Phone a Friend (Team):** You grab a teammate before walking in: *"I need to tag you in. If I present solo, there's a real risk of error. Can you be my second set of eyes or co-presenter? I need backup."*
- **Leader Escalation (if needed):** If no teammate can step in, you own it with the board chair: *"We're pausing here. These numbers are too critical to rush through at 25%. I'd rather delay twenty minutes and get it right than risk damaging confidence."*
- **Micro-Boundary:** You renegotiate in the moment, delay the meeting, redistribute presentation sections, or adjust the delivery format.

Micro-Boundary (When You Can't Delay or Call Backup)

Sometimes you don't have a second chair. Sometimes the boardroom is full, the clock is ticking, and there's no one to tag in. In those moments, the micro-boundary looks different.

You shift the frame for your audience. You don't need to say, "I'm 25/Red"; they don't know the H.E.A.R.T. language. But you can buy yourself space and manage expectations with phrases like:

- *"I want to make sure I cover this clearly. Let me anchor us on the top three takeaways first."*
- *"I'll keep this concise, and we'll follow up with details in writing after."*
- *"This is a critical conversation. If I miss something in real time, I'll circle back by the end of the day."*

The key is that you narrow the aperture. You don't try to give them everything. You set boundaries around what you can do well in this moment.

- **Pin:** Later, you note that the failure point wasn't just low energy; it was structural. Too much rested on one person. That insight becomes a systemic fix for next time.

The key lesson: Sometimes a red flag means stop. Not just tether. Not just boundary. Stop. Phone a friend. Pull a lever. Push the deadline. Because protecting both the system and yourself matters more than powering through at 25%.

Behind the scenes, that's the red flag in action, protecting the integrity of the work while protecting yourself. You aren't hiding weakness; you're modeling clarity under pressure. And ironically, most boards and executives respect that more than someone powering through at half capacity and making avoidable mistakes.

Red-Flag Protocol in Action

In startup land, you're always fundraising. No matter how much you've raised, it never feels like enough. You're hunting for the right partner, the right investor who brings not just money but network, expertise, and a proven track record of building alongside their portfolio companies.

And if you've ever raised money, you know it's anything but fun. You show up with an idea, a strategy, a stack of spreadsheets, and a dream. Recently, I read *Pour Your Heart Into It,* where Starbucks CEO Howard Schultz shared that he pitched to 274 investors. Two hundred seventeen gave him an immediate no. Imagine that. Even the most resilient founder, burning

The Red-Flag Protocol

with energy and conviction, would start to buckle under that rejection.

The hardest part? Investor meetings are high-stakes moments. No second chances. No do-overs. No ability to say, "Sorry, I'm having a bad day. I actually know this inside out, but I'm exhausted." The exhaustion shows. Investors don't just bet on your ideas or unit economics; they bet on you. They bet on your energy, resilience, authenticity, and how you show up in the room.

I've been fortunate to cofound alongside someone with incredible emotional intelligence. She's detail-oriented, deeply prepared, and reads a room better than almost anyone I've ever seen. Before every investor call, we'd run through the flow, who would say what, how we'd transition, and how we'd show we were a polished, aligned team.

But there was one call, after months of travel and long days getting our first hub off the ground, when I simply didn't have 100 percent to give. My battery was drained. I was road-weary. And the pressure of "this one really counts" weighed heavy.

Without missing a beat, she adjusted. I opened with introductions since the relationship had started with me. Then she took the lead, carrying the bulk of the conversation and sharing our mission, vision, and energy flawlessly. I chimed in where it made sense, but she held the weight of the call. We never discussed it, never planned it. She just knew.

Looking back, knowing what I know now, I would have called the Red-Flag Protocol that morning. I would have told the team, *"I'm running low today, and I need backup."* Because not every teammate reads a room that well. Not every team has years of built-in trust.

The gift she gave me that day was more than carrying the call. It was the feeling of being seen, valued, and supported. No strings attached. No judgment. Just care.

And that's what the Red-Flag Protocol creates when practiced intentionally: a culture where people can be honest about their limits without putting the mission at risk. A culture where teammates step in for each other without hesitation. A culture where being human isn't a liability but an advantage.

Because when we protect each other in the hard moments, everybody wins.

Saying No

The H.E.A.R.T. Check works best when it becomes a shared practice. When the whole team speaks the same language, it creates alignment, safety, and consistency. No one feels singled out, and no one gets left guessing.

But what if you're the only one ready to try?

Start by finding out who on your team is open to it. You don't need everyone on day one; you just need a few willing partners who see the value. Begin small, build consistency, and let others see the impact over time. Momentum grows when people notice how much more supported and aligned you feel.

Even if your team isn't fully ready, you can still use the H.E.A.R.T. Check for yourself. Self-awareness, tethering, and micro-boundaries work powerfully at the individual level. But for the system to deliver its full benefit, for burnout to be caught early, for trust to deepen, and for common language to actually *stick*, the more people on board, the better it works.

Part of making the H.E.A.R.T. Check work is remembering that **participation is always a choice**. If someone asks, "Do you want to check in today?" you're always allowed to say **no**. And no is a complete sentence.

We want to build cultures where people feel safe enough to share, where H.E.A.R.T. becomes part of the rhythm of daily work, not a burden. But honoring the whole person means honoring boundaries too. Some days, the most authentic check-in is simply passing.

When "no" is respected without pushback, it strengthens trust. It shows that participation is an invitation, never an obligation, and that's what makes people more likely to say "yes" when they're ready.

It doesn't mean:

- *Ask me again in five minutes.*
- *Press me for why I don't want to share.*
- *Assume something is wrong.*

It simply means no right now. That's it.

Respecting a no is just as important as respecting a yes. True psychological safety includes the freedom to opt out. When people know you'll honor their boundaries, they're actually more likely to lean in when they're ready.

Here's some language you can use if you want to decline:

- "No thanks, not today."
- "I'm going to pass on this one."
- "I don't want to check in right now."

And the only correct response from the other side is:

- "Got it."
- "Thanks for letting us know."

When It Doesn't Click with Everyone, Remember It Is For YOU!

Sometimes you'll try these tools and they won't resonate with your team. You'll run a Red-Flag Protocol, and no one will step in. You'll feel like you're carrying the weight alone. That happens, and it doesn't mean the practice isn't worth it.

If I'd had these tools years ago, if I'd given myself permission to check in daily with my own battery through the H.E.A.R.T. Check-in, I would have caught the signs of burnout long before it was too late. I know the exact moment when it tipped for me.

I had just driven my beloved electric truck, Bob, up the Grapevine in California in the middle of summer. The truck was only partially charged when I picked it up, which meant hours of detours, sitting in Denny's parking lots while charging, and watching my delivery deadline slip further away. I hate overpromising and underdelivering, but that day the universe had other plans.

Somewhere between the truck's big windows giving me a sunburn, the third charging station that wouldn't work, and a conference call that dragged on while my battery dwindled, I hit 5 percent Red, discouraged, angry, and bone tired.

Then, out of nowhere, a stranger walked up. He was also a founder, retrofitting box trucks to be electric. He moved his vehicle so I could charge mine, sat with me in the sweltering heat, and swapped war stories about startup life. He missed his kid's birthday that day; I was six hours late to my customer. But in those thirty minutes of real human connection, my battery recharged in a way no nap or power outlet could. Before he left, he handed me a cold bottle of water. We've stayed connected ever since.

I'll never forget how burned out I was, or how much that one moment of empathy mattered. For the next year and a half, I pushed at 150 percent, through exhaustion and through those "zero battery" moments, because I didn't want to let my team down. But I stayed burned out the entire time. If I had known then what I know now, how to name my battery level, how to tether when I was running low, or how to use common language to ask for help, I would have caught it sooner. I would have been healthier, and my work would have been stronger.

So if you're doing this work and it feels like you're the only one, remember this: you're not doing it wrong. You're doing it for you. You're building awareness, language, and tools that become a gift you carry forward, no matter who joins you. And sometimes, like that stranger at the charging station, the universe will send someone to remind you that you're not alone.

Net Effect: These scripts give people the words to actually run the protocol. The extreme case shows that honoring red flags isn't about fragility; it's about protecting the business from crisis.

Chapter 6: The Red-Flag Protocol

What's one red flag I ignored recently, and what did it cost me or my team?

_____
_____
_____
_____
_____
_____
_____
_____
_____
_____

How would it feel to have permission to pause and reset before the damage is done?

_____
_____
_____
_____

CHAPTER 7

Culture: The Symphony or the Noise

There are companies where culture feels like an invisible current pulling people forward. Hilton. Costco. Wegmans. Google. Toyota. These aren't just brands with good perks; they're operating systems.

At Hilton, frontline employees are trusted and empowered to solve problems on the spot, with clear career pathways built into the system. At Wegmans, employees describe community and belonging as the heart of their experience, while leadership frames employee happiness as the engine driving customer loyalty. Costco built its model on the "good jobs strategy," higher pay, better benefits, and predictable schedules, keeping turnover around 8 percent in an industry where 60 percent is the norm. Google's Project Aristotle revealed that psychological safety is the number one predictor of effective teams. Netflix codified "freedom and responsibility" into its operating system, building high-talent density by replacing control with context. Toyota's lean culture proved that "respect for people and continuous improvement" could scale globally, transforming factory floors into innovation hubs.

These cultures aren't about perks. They're about trust, safety, belonging, and alignment. They boost effort, invite ideas, and strengthen retention. The numbers prove it:

- Companies on the Fortune 100 Best Companies to Work For list (built from more than 1.3 million survey responses) have outperformed the S&P 500 by 3.5 times over the past 27 years.
- Gallup research shows that engaged, culture-aligned employees drive 14 percent higher productivity, 21 percent higher profitability, and significantly lower absenteeism and turnover.
- MIT's Culture 500 found that toxic culture is 10.4 times more predictive of attrition than pay, proving that what people feel day to day matters far more than what's on their paycheck.

Culture isn't soft. It's compounding cash flow.

When the Storm Hit

In 2017, a call went out within our organization, an industrial staffing company, asking for volunteers to help with Hurricane Harvey. At the time, I held a senior leadership role in national account management, overseeing customer segments from hospitality to transportation and everything in between. I wasn't involved in day-to-day branch operations, so it might have seemed unusual for me to answer the call. But I felt strongly that I could make an impact. I had always been the one sitting in meetings after storms, reviewing revenue spikes, cost impacts, and customer reports. This time, I wanted to see for myself what really happened on the ground and maybe, just maybe, make a difference.

If you've never stepped into a region hit by a mass disaster, it's an experience that stays with you forever. There's a smell you can't quite identify, devastation on every corner, and a heaviness in the air that feels thicker than humidity. Harvey left its mark on my heart just as it did on so many others.

We were fortunate that our branch still had power. On my very first day, I arrived to find people wrapped around the building. These were men and women whose regular jobs had vanished overnight, but they still wanted, needed, to work. They had families to feed. And that's what we did best: we put people to work and got them paid the same day so they could put food on the table that night. It was transactional, yes, but it was also profoundly human.

During Harvey, I spent my days checking crews on worksites and making sure branch employees had what they needed: printers, supplies, the basics that keep operations running. Midway through my seven-day stretch, I learned that one of our customer service reps had a birthday the next day. Her home was flooded. She walked through waist-deep water every morning just to reach the branch because she knew how much the workers relied on her to keep things moving. So I picked up a birthday cake, and we celebrated right there in the middle of chaos. I'll never forget her tears of gratitude. That small moment of joy, carved out of loss and exhaustion, reminded me that culture isn't measured in memos or financial reports. It's measured in whether people feel seen and supported when everything else is falling apart.

That week gave me a new lens and forced me to ask hard human questions. How do we support branch employees who themselves lost homes and belongings? Do we provide clean clothes and personal essentials so they can show up with dignity? Do we fly in volunteers from other regions if it means taking up scarce hotel space that locals desperately need? How do we get supplies to the right places when the infrastructure is broken? These weren't questions on our quarterly reports, but they were the ones that mattered most to the people holding the company together.

The Revenue Reality

Here's the other side of the story: Hurricane Harvey became a massive moneymaker for us. In just four months, we logged more than $11 million in top-line revenue. These catastrophic events always spiked our numbers, and leadership loved it. But here's the culture problem: from a revenue management perspective, you can't control hurricanes. You can't manufacture one. And you definitely can't control where they hit.

Still, leadership expected the same thing every year: double-digit growth. After Harvey's windfall, when the following year rolled around, they expected us to hit those same numbers in the same regions. I remember laughing and saying, "I can't manufacture a hurricane."

But no one else laughed.

Reporting honestly about business realities wasn't safe. The culture rewarded denial and punished transparency. When expectations disconnect from reality, culture collapses.

The cultural issues that surfaced during these storm events went far deeper than revenue reports. They created burnout. One of our top national account managers, someone responsible for an entire vertical and critical customer relationships, walked away just six months after the 2017 storm season ended. She didn't leave because of the work itself, but because of the lack of support and unrealistic revenue expectations. She spent eight years fighting an uphill battle, growing her vertical from $7 million to $26 million in annual revenue. While storms might return the following year, everyone knew the odds of forecasting when and where were slim.

A healthier culture would have looked different. It would have acknowledged the percentage of revenue tied to storm recovery and set honest goals for how we would make up the difference in other areas. That would have been alignment. That would have been honesty. That would have been leadership. Instead, we got unrealistic pressure, burnout, and eventually turnover from the very people we needed most.

That moment made it clear to me that culture isn't what you say in a town hall or hang on a wall. It's how you respond in the hard seasons, when honesty is inconvenient and humanity costs time and resources.

What Culture Really Is

Culture isn't the ping-pong table. It isn't free coffee. It's not the motivational town hall.

By definition:

- **Formal:** Company culture is the shared values, beliefs, norms, and behaviors that shape how work gets done and how people interact inside an organization.
- **Plain English:** Culture is "how we do things around here." All the time, during the good, the bad, and the ugly.

It's invisible but deeply felt. It shows up in:

- **Values** → what gets rewarded and what gets tolerated.
- **Norms** → the unwritten rules: how meetings run, how people give feedback, how teams handle conflict.
- **Behaviors** → daily actions, from frontline employees to executives.
- **Stories & Symbols** → the rituals, language, and narratives that reinforce what truly matter.
- **Systems** → hiring, recognition, and promotion processes that either strengthen or weaken culture.

Culture serves as both the glue that binds people together and the grease that makes work flow smoothly. When done well, it creates a symphony where everyone plays in sync. When done poorly, it generates noise, constant friction, wasted energy, and missed potential.

Why Leaders Can't Leave Culture to Chance

The best leaders don't hope culture happens. They intentionally design it and fiercely protect it.

Because they understand:

- High trust drives greater effort, better ideas, and stronger retention.
- Psychological safety unlocks innovation.
- Fair treatment and dignity boost both productivity and loyalty.
- Clarity and alignment reduce waste, errors, and rework.

Culture isn't "nice to have." It's the compound interest on every choice leaders make when no one's watching.

The Takeaway

The best cultures, Hilton, Costco, Wegmans, Google, and Toyota, aren't built on perks; they're operating systems. They cultivate trust and psychological safety, which drive effort, spark ideas, and retain talent. The results speak for themselves: +21% profitability, lower turnover, and decades of market outperformance, averaging about +6% per year over the S&P. Culture isn't soft; it's compounding cash flow.

The strongest company cultures already run on trust, safety, and alignment, but **Lead with Heart** helps them shine even brighter. And for a company that doesn't yet have a top-tier culture, Lead with Heart can help you start the journey to a better place. You don't need board approval or a corporate rollout to begin. Culture shifts the moment people do.

Start with your peers, your team, and your daily check-ins. Begin today. Even when you think no one is watching, they are, and the ripple effect will spread. Small, human choices compound over time. That's how symphonies get written, and that's how cultures transform.

Take It to Heart Chapter 7: Culture: The Symphony or the Noise

If culture is "how we do things around here," what would someone really say about ours?

_____
_____
_____
_____
_____
_____
_____

What's one daily action I could take to shift the noise toward symphony?

_____
_____
_____
_____
_____
_____
_____
_____

CHAPTER 8

Making It Stick and Measuring What Matters

Tools don't change culture. Consistent practice does.

Over the years, whether in Fortune 500 boardrooms, consulting on transformation projects, or building my own startups, I've witnessed the same pattern repeatedly. Organizations get excited about a new idea, system, or program, but then it fades into background noise. Great intentions, zero staying power.

Why? Because the gap between "a great idea" and "sustained advantage" comes down to rhythm. Rhythm emerges from two essential elements: **consistent practice and visible measurement**.

If you only implement without measuring, people eventually wonder, *"But is this actually working?"* If you only measure without implementing, you create dashboards full of theory with no real behavior behind them. When you combine both, you create culture change that's both human and profitable.

Why Measurement Matters (ROI Lens)

Culture isn't soft. Culture compounds into cash flow.

If we believe people are the business, then happier, better-aligned humans stay longer, innovate more, serve customers better, and make smarter decisions. That impact shows up directly on your bottom line.

To prove it, you have to measure what matters. Not everything, not the 47 KPIs your organization already tracks, just the five metrics that consistently reveal whether your people and business are thriving. These aren't random; they're the benchmarks every boardroom, every executive team, and every founder I've ever worked with comes back to, no matter the size of the company. They are the universal barometers of success:

1. **Revenue – Are you growing?** Revenue is the most visible signal of business momentum. Without growth, everything else stalls.
2. **Profitability – Are you sustainable?** Growth without profit is a treadmill; it burns energy but doesn't last. Profitability is proof that the model works.

3. **Cash Flow – Can you survive unexpected shocks?** Cash flow is oxygen. Without it, even the best business suffocates in the short term.
4. **Customer Metrics – Retention, satisfaction, Net Promoter Score.** Customers are your proof point in the market. If they're leaving, unhappy, or not advocating for you, growth is a mirage.
5. **Employee Engagement & Retention – Can you keep delivering with your current team?** People carry the business forward. If they're burned out, leaving, or disengaged, performance crumbles no matter what your revenue line says.

They may call them different things, but they always show up because they tell the story of health, resilience, and future potential. That's why they matter.

Take a snapshot today. Lock it in. That's your baseline. Then track monthly for at least six months. Six months matters because the first few weeks feel clunky, like exercising any new muscle. You need enough runway to spot a genuine trend, not just a temporary blip.

And if things aren't moving as expected, ask the hard question: Are we actually using the Lead with Heart tools, or did we just read about them once and hope for magic?

How to Make It Stick (Implementation Lens)

Here's the part people often skip: you can have the world's best framework, but if you don't weave it into daily operations, it evaporates.

The most effective implementation strategies aren't complicated. They're:

- **Simple & Visible.** A two-minute H.E.A.R.T. Check with shared language: Battery, Tether, Pin, (Black Bag). Actions people can see and repeat.
- **Tracked.** Visible metrics tied to real priorities. When the line moves, the culture feels it.
- **Scalable.** Start small. Pilot with one leader, one team, one project. Adjust, then grow.
- **Owned.** Everyone plays a role. Individuals log batteries, leaders protect time, and teams run check-ins.
- **Protected.** Reflection and alignment time are non-negotiable. Leaders defend it as they would a revenue meeting.

What It Looks Like in Real Life

Day 1: A leader runs a private H.E.A.R.T. Check and blocks 15 minutes for reflection.

Week 1: They introduce it to their team: "Quick check: Battery %, one emotion word." It takes two minutes. People feel awkward but curious.

Month 1: Someone uses the Red-Flag Protocol mid-meeting when energy dips. The reset happens faster than anyone expects.

Month 2: A simple dashboard goes live, showing revenue trends, engagement pulse, and customer Net Promoter Score. Everyone can see progress in real time.

Quarter 1: Error rates drop, retention climbs, and people report fewer "energy crashes." The numbers match the mood.

Quarter 2: Other teams start asking, "What are you doing differently?" The practice begins scaling naturally.

The Bottom Line

Implementation without measurement is noise. Measurement without implementation is empty. Together, they create rhythm.

- Simple language.
- Visible rituals.
- Protected time.
- Numbers that show the line is moving.

That's how Lead with Heart goes from being "a great idea" to the way we do things around here. It works for the humans. It works for the business. And you'll have the data to prove it.

When you do that consistently, Lead with Heart doesn't just exist in your organization; it lives in it.

Take It to Heart Chapter 8: *Implementing Lead with Heart*

Where could I start small, one team, one ritual, one metric, instead of waiting for a perfect rollout?

_____
_____
_____
_____
_____

What would success look like in 90 days if we began now?

_____
_____
_____
_____
_____

Just the Beginning

Sometimes the end of a book is just... the end. A neat conclusion, a bow on top, a full stop.

But I hope that for you, this marks only the beginning.

I hope you've seen things through a different lens. I hope you've discovered a fresh perspective, experienced a few "aha" moments, and feel inspired to put this into practice, whether as an individual, with your direct reports, or across your entire leadership team.

I hope you now understand what I had to learn the hard way: the people doing the work are complete human beings. They're not just numbers, not just job titles, not just producers of output. They carry their lives, dreams, struggles, and joy into the workplace with them. When we create systems that honor the whole person, the business thrives. Lower turnover. Reduced burnout. Higher profits. Stronger culture.

We've explored the hole in the floor, those hidden costs that slowly drain organizations. Let's close by looking at what preventative maintenance actually means.

I love a good car analogy, so here's one from the garage: imagine buying a Honda built to last 350,000 miles, but you never change the oil. The warning light flashes, and you ignore it. Eventually, the engine seizes on the side of the road, leaving you standing there, bewildered, wondering what went wrong.

That's exactly how too many companies treat their people. They expect long-term performance without providing basic care and maintenance for the humans who power the business. Lead with Heart means putting oil in the engine. It means paying attention when the check-engine light comes on. It means building a culture where caring for people isn't an add-on; it's fundamental.

And here's the beautiful part: when you invest in people, the business doesn't just perform better. The people flourish too. Even when they move on, they leave stronger.

Imagine having a culture where you could say, *"Jerry may have left to pursue another opportunity, but while he was here, he made incredible contributions. We're better for it. And so is he."*

Because that's legacy. That's culture. That's leadership.

If you're reading this as an individual, pause and check in with yourself. Notice your energy levels. When you're running low, tether yourself to what matters. Create a micro-boundary. Remember that no state lasts forever; this too shall pass.

If you're a leader, use this system to align your team, getting everyone paddling in the same direction. You'll move faster than competing boats, not because you demand it, but because your people feel energized, connected, and genuinely cared for.

If you're a CEO, this doesn't have to become another book you read and forget. It can become the framework that finally bridges culture and results. You don't have to choose between people and profit. When you lead with heart, you achieve both.

Now it's time to put this into action. Revisit the tools, lean on the protocols, and use the language. Remember, the veil of forgetfulness is real. Competing priorities will always tug at your attention. But if you return to these practices daily, weekly, and consistently, they'll become second nature.

This isn't the end; it's the beginning of a new way of working. A way that honors the whole person, drives business success, and leaves the world better than we found it.

Lead with heart. Always.

Take it to Heart Closing: *Just the Beginning*

How will I keep this system from becoming "just another book I read"?

_____
_____
_____
_____
_____
_____
_____

Who will I invite to take this journey with me, so it sticks?

_____
_____
_____
_____
_____
_____
_____
_____
_____

www.ingramcontent.com/pod-product-compliance
Lightning Source LLC
Chambersburg PA
CBHW072049160426
43197CB00014B/2690